olivia eloise seve

deeper you dig,
darker it gets

deeper you dig, darker it gets

olivia eloise sever

to my past self
for closing this chapter of your life

to my future self
i hope you're still here

to whoever holding this in your hands
i love you

deeper you dig, darker it gets

olivia eloise sever

**this collection of work contains
the following content warnings
please stay safe and
please stay mindful of your limits**

mental health conditions
emotional & verbal abuse
self-harm
suicide
eating disorders
body dysmorphia
death/grief

deeper you dig, darker it gets

truth of me

i don't have any experience
with boys or girls.
i've never had a
real interest in anyone.
a superficial crush
here or there,
but nothing heartfelt.

so i can't write
lines and lines
of poetry that dictate
the highs and lows
of my love life.
cause i simply
haven't had one.

but i can give you
pages and pages
filled with words
that are true.
ones that tell
you about me.
the sad,
the angry,
the grieving.
cause that's who i am
that's what makes me,
me.

a slap in the face

it simply hits you,
like a slap in the face,
one day you're
doing great
and have support.

the next,
your whole world
is crumbling,
almost as fast
as you are
and there is no one
there to help
pick up the pieces.

yet it's not as
instantaneous as it seems.
people merely fall away,
like leaves off trees
as summer
turns to winter.

and one day,
you open your eyes
and realize
all you are left with
are bare branches
stuck out in the cold.
to freeze,
utterly
and completely
alone.

olivia eloise sever

a positive thought?

i'm not perfect,
i'm far from it.

i'm mean.
i pick at my face.
i weigh too much.
i don't fit clothes properly.
i'm sad
and rude.
i eat too much,
don't sleep enough.
my hair never sits just right.
i have dirt under my nails
and i slouch when i sit.

i'm not perfect,
i'm the furthest thing from it.
yet no one is perfect,
no matter how hard they try.

i'm fine

i feel like
i'm making everything up.
that i'm faking it.
that none of it's true.
it's all an act,
that i'm being overdramatic.
i'm completely fine.
i'm just being a brat.

it's not like
i'm cutting so deep
i'm in need
of stitches.

it's not like
i'm starving myself
to the point
of just bones.

i was never physically
hurt as a kid.
i have a caring family
and i'm not being bullied

the attempts i've made
have never succeeded.
the role i've played
has left me defeated.

i'm just waiting everyone's time.
i'm just making it all up.
i'm fine.

tea and princesses

long gone is the girl
who played princess
and threw tea parties.

forgive and forget

she hurt me,
i can't forgive her.
or at least not yet
but i will never forget.

i will never forget
how she took away my comfort.
i will never forget
how she manipulated my beliefs.
i will never forget
how she tried to make me hate him.

but most of all
i will never forget
how she was once
my favourite person,
my hero,
my mother.

olivia eloise sever

a failed escape

there's a cloaked figure
at the end of the hall.
just for a moment
neither one of us moves.

suddenly it darts forward,
advancing on me
at a ridiculous speed.

i run till my lungs burn,
the soules of my shoes
barely hitting the ground
beneath me as
i race to escape its
dangerous claws.

though my efforts
are in vain.
the thing on my tale
seems to know
the terrain better than i do.

before i can comprehend
what has happened,
i lay flat on the floor.
the hot breath of a creature
breathing down my neck.

in a last attempt to escape,
i use all my weight
to flip us over.

we were, now we aren't

you were always there,
now you're not.

we always talked,
now we don't.

we were best friends,
now we aren't.

you were my light,
now i'm stuck in the dark.

i loved you with my whole heart,
i never stopped.

olivia eloise sever

jumble from my nonfunctioning brain

i don't know how to think anymore.
i don't know how to cry anymore.

i'm confused,
everything is all jumbled.
i try to think,
yet a thought will not form.
it's all just fuzzy
as if a connection has been severed.

i try to cry,
yet i physically can't shed a tear.
no matter how upset,
no matter how hurt,
my eyes remain dry.

i don't know how to think anymore.
i don't know how to cry anymore.

a daughter and her mother: such a complex thing

i am my mother's daughter.
no matter how much
i wish it weren't so.
no matter how much
i try to deny it.
i truly am my mother's daughter.

i have an explosive temper,
just like her.
i hurt people around me,
just like her.
i am my own worst enemy,
just like her.

the more i grow up,
the more i realize,
that my nightmare
is becoming a reality.
i am exactly like her.
i am my mother's daughter.

tale of a monster

i am a monster
in my own right.
i've done
things i'm not
proud of.
i've spoken words
i wish i could
take back.

haunting thoughts
keep me up in the night.
ones i would
never share with
another soul.

actions i've taken
derived from hate
instead of love.
i wish never to have
to think of again.

phrases shouted
in the form of
an attack.
so vicious and vile
the devil himself
would be offended.

it could easily be
spun into a tale
of warning
you tell your children.

deeper you dig, darker it gets

watch your words.
watch your actions.
don't become a monster.

everyone reaches they're breaking point

i've been trying
for so long.

'keep your head up.'
'put a smile on your face.'
'act as if you're great.'

but i'm not great.
or good.
or okay.
or fine.

i'm *tired.*

tired of the crick in my neck.
of lips cracking till they bled.
of the constant mask stuck to my face.

i'm tired of living a lie.
of always trying,
yet always breaking.
of having every step i take
crumble beneath my weight.

i'm falling into darkness,
never to be seen again.
at least it would
finally be the end.

deeper you dig, darker it gets

i am deserving

i deserve this,
all of this.
every excruciating,
agonizing,
bit of it.

i'm a piece of shit.
a worthless,
pathetic,
excuse for
a human.

all the pain
i've felt,
the sorrow
i've suffered through,
it's warranted.
it's justified.
it's deserved.

a daughter

my eyes sting
as tears stream
down my face
dripping onto the bedding.
your bedding.

i watch wide eyed,
ringing in my ears
as you turn your back
and walk out the door.
your door.

what did i do
to deserve this?
am i really so broken
even you can't love me?
is this how you're meant
to treat a daughter?
your daughter.

art of harm

scars litter my arms,
lines cover my thighs.
each one carved with precision.
watchful eyes observe the repetition.
red runs down,
dripping,
dripping,
hitting the ground.
the numbness follows
and sleep comes till the next tomorrow.

olivia eloise sever

despair

i live in a pit
of my own doing.
full of pop cans
and empty wrappers.
a never-ending hole
pulling me down
deeper into my own despair.

free?

freedom.
isn't that what we all want in this world,
isn't that the end goal?
freedom to make our own choices,
our own decisions,
our own actions.

yet are we ever truly free?
shackled down by socialite rules.
expectations put before us
since childhood.
assumptions made by others,
strangers even.

so are we ever truly free?
what about from ourselves?
our thoughts,
anxieties,
fears,
ambitions?

is it keeping you
from what they call
your true potential?
or is this all you were meant for?
is this as far as you go?
is this as free as you get?

olivia eloise sever

a letter to the grave

dear mom,

loving you has always been hard.
and sometimes i wish i didn't have to.
though missing you is even worse.
cause no matter my feelings,
i'll never see you again.

most of all i mourn
what was and what could've been.
the untainted memories from when i was a girl.
the relationship we might've been able to rebuild.

not what i had,
not who i had.
the yelling and the crying and the guilt tripping.
the woman who should've gotten help
before becoming a mother.

cause a child can't fix your problems
and all it brings is more pain.

maybe in another world,
neither one of us would have to of suffered.
you could've been good and found love.
maybe you would've had me
or maybe you wouldn't of.
but you could've been happy, *alive.*

it's too late now.
you're gone, dead, no longer living.
and i envy you because of it.

you caused as much pain as you felt.
but never took responsibility.
it was always someone else's fault.

'the abused become the abuser' right?
but you could've fought that.
or at least of tried.
and if i wasn't worth it,
if i wasn't motivation enough,
you should've done it for yourself.

cause maybe,
possibly,
you could've seen the error of your ways
and i'd still have a mother.

— your daughter

five

five cuts and you're done
i tell myself.
stick to five.
five is just enough.
five is all i need.
oh,
but look.
a sixth,
a seventh,
and an eighth, ninth, tenth…

with me

a shadow
followed me
for so long.
i paid it
no mind.
it was simply
with me as i
got through
the day.

it started to
darken and drag.
i did not let myself
be concerned.
it was simply
with me as i
fought through
the day.

it grew larger
and stronger.
i merely ignored
the change.
it was simply
with me as i
forgot about
the day.

olivia eloise sever

gone

now that she's gone
i don't know what to do.
the guilt,
the sadness,
the relief,
the memories,
the good & the bad.

the ones where we'd
talk about the future.
me getting married,
having kids,
wedding dress shopping,
baby names,
graduation,
trips.
i know she won't be there for any of it.

the ones where she'd get upset
with me over anything,
everything.
screaming,
yelling,
tears running down my face.
i know she can't hurt me anymore.

she's gone.
i know she's gone.
yet she stays with me,
in the best and the worst.
forever.

the call that was silenced

it truly started as
a cry for help,
a way to prove
how badly i was hurting.

but i underestimated
how good it would feel
and how addictive
it would become.

it turned into a way
for the pain to be real
and not just some chemical imbalance
hidden in my brain.

the silence that followed
simply added to the appeal.
the hurt made the voices go quiet,
even for a moment.

soon i did all i could
to keep it concealed.
i no longer wanted
people to know.

it became my little secret,
tucked away under my sleeves,
the fabric muffling what was
once a cry for help,
that now was no longer
meant to be seen.

ballad of the dead mother

'i'm sorry but your mother has passed away'
'w-what?'

i took a step back
as my knees buckled
and i fell to the ground.
someone's arms caught me,
one person in front, one behind.
my nails dug into the dirt,
ripping out the dry grass
as my hands were grabbed by another's.

'no. no, i loved her!
she didn't know i loved her!'

'oh, sweetie, yes, yes she did.
i promise she knew.'
'no, no, no, she thought i hated her!'

screams were torn from my mouth,
catching the attention
of the people around us,
but i did not care.
a person leaves,
but is quickly replaced.

all the while
the tears did not stop.
they flowed rapidly
down my cheeks,
soaking the collar of my shirt.
my throat became raw

but my yells did not stop.
i couldn't wrap my mind around it.

this can't be happening,
this can't be happening,
i didn't get to say goodbye.
she can't be gone.

but she is.

pleading with the universe

yelling rattles within my brain,
taking me back to a time
i wish i could not remember.

fear courses through my veins.
tears gather in my eyes.

make it stop.
please make it stop.
get me out of here.
GET ME OUT.

no matter what i try,
i'm stuck in a loop
of cruel voices
and heinous accusations.

i want out.
i don't want to be here anymore.

hands clamped over my ears,
hidden beneath a blanket.

please...
please get me out.
please.

distant memory

the image of her smile
disappears.
the tone of her laugh
grows less clear.
the memories of how
she'd say my name
begin to fade
and everyday i am
reminded that eventually
i'll have spent more time
with her gone
then with her near.

simplicity of dying

i want to die.

i don't have
any clever analogies,
or beautiful rhymes,
or a nice way to say it.

i simply want to die.

the wanting

there is no way
to sugarcoat
wanting to die.

no fancy way
to say it,
to soften the blow.
believe me,
i've tried.

there is no perfect
way to describe
the whole in my chest
or the thoughts in my head.

there is merely the truth.
my brain is trying to kill me,
and i'm more than happy to let it continue.

olivia eloise sever

darling little girl

i am so sorry my little darling.
you deserved so much more.
to feel appreciated
and celebrated.
to have been taken care of
and comforted.
to have played with friends
and made long-lasting
memories.

that's what childhood is.
and that's what you
should have lived.
not what you actually did.

you shouldn't have been
mature for your age.
or beg to be loved.
you shouldn't have had
to heal her,
while ignoring the reasons
not to forgive her.

a weight was put on
your shoulders when
you were far too young
and there was no one there
to share it with.

oh my little darling,
you deserved so much more,
i wish i could say it gets better.

food: the mortal enemy of the teenage girl

i eat when i'm hungry.
i eat when i'm bored.
i eat when i'm sad.
i eat whenever i can.

i always regret
what i ate.
all it does is
fuel the hate
i hold against myself.

each bite i take
adds to the pounds
around my waist.
i can't stop it,
can't control it,
no matter how much
i wish i could quit.

tale of a panic attack

hands muffle my cries
as i push myself
further into the corner
hoping it will
swallow me whole.

pain radiates through my chest
as my throat starts to close.

i can't breathe
why can't i breathe

i think maybe
this will be the end.
maybe this is
when i finally die.
that what i've been praying for
for so long finally comes true.

but then
air enters my lungs.
and i can breathe again.

paradise or sacrifice

since i was young
i've been taught
that when i die,
i'll go to heaven.

that it's a place
of peace and happiness.
so utterly perfect
you can do no wrong.

so i pose this question.
why should i continue
to live in a place
where all i've received
is pain and suffering?
where all i've done
is cause problems?

when the alternative is
paradise.

olivia eloise sever

random brain spew

how could you
do it all so easily,
so casually cruel
and uncaring.

ignoring the
catastrophe
you left in
your path.

deeper you dig, darker it gets

sad stains

reminders of my pain
will forever stain
my body.

absquatulate

to leave without saying goodbye.
guilt remaining long thereafter.
the last bit of warmth.
the last fragment of sound.
fading in to the background.
leaving nothing but sorrow behind.

a man whose name is death

i wonder if death
is ever happy?
i wonder if he feels?
was he once a man
like the rest of us,
before he was
given a terrible
burden to bear.
or was he always
the skeleton with
a cloak we see
depicted in pictures.

maybe he wears
the hood because
he's ashamed
of how he looks.
or maybe he wears it
to strike fear
into his victims.

i guess we'll never know.
but i'd really like to meet him.
i have a few questions.

story of a failed friendship

once upon a time
lived a young girl
and her best friend.

they laughed till
their stomachs hurt.
never seen without
one another.
the orange penguins
they called themselves.

she lived in a fantasy world,
they'd be friends forever,
they'd never be apart,
they'd grow old together.
oh how naïve she was.

they grew up
and the fairytale dissolved.
before she knew it
the laughter stopped
and it'd be months since
she'd last seen them.

they moved on
and made new friends.
she was left behind,
clinging to the scraps
of their intertwined past.
stuck alone dealing with
her own inner demons.

though she can't
hold it against them.
she would've done the same.
she's happy for them,
she wishes them the best,
she just wishes she was less depressed.

in the end,
one lived happily ever after,
while the other was stuck
lost in a disaster.

olivia eloise sever

truth in grieving

when people die
it's often believed
there comes a time
where one must
'move on'
or
'get over it'
that you must
live your life
like it never happened.

but truly
it's not something you
'move on from'
or
'get over'
it's something you must
learn to live with.

yes, it's painful.
unbearable.
it hurts,
day in
and
day out.
it won't ever go away,
but with time
it'll lessen.

and one day
you'll realize that
that excruciating pain

deeper you dig, darker it gets

you once felt
will be but
a dull ache
lost in your chest

mirror, mirror on the wall, oh how badly i want to smash thee

i can't look in
a mirror anymore,
too disgusted by
what's in front of me.
i'm moments away from
shattering the glass,
so i no longer have to see
the horrid human
staring back at me.

my stomach sticks out
farther than it should
and i wish i could take
scissors to my skin.
marking out with a pen
what i want gone
and simply cutting
it all away.

i'd rather stand
in front of a mirror,
bloody and scarred,
then how i am now,
ugly and large.

screaming thoughts

i used to fall asleep
to the sound of fighting
right outside my door.

i still do,
in a way.
yet it's no longer
on the other side of the door.
it's a lot closer to home,
more private,
but no less tormenting.
it echoes through my head,
my thoughts screaming
at one another.

more vicious than
whatever somebody else
could throw at me.
more damaging than
whatever insults were
being exchanged across the room
on the other side of the wall.

olivia eloise sever

9 years of age

no one ever talks about
how i almost died at 9.

everyone has moved on,
except me, apparently.

they all came out unscathed
while my life was forever changed.

seventeen

17
what a strange
age to be.

you'd like to think
you know everything
but in reality
you know nothing.

you want to be
treated like an adult
yet you still
feel like a kid.

i never thought
i'd make it to
my 17th birthday.
i truly thought
i'd be dead
by then.

and yet
i made it.

but as i look back
i regret every moment
it took to get here.
every day spent
in pain and sorrow,
every day trying
to stay strong,
thinking i'd ever

olivia eloise sever

get the chance
to get better.

it simply was
not worth it
and i wish
i'd never done it.
i wish i never made it to 17.

deeper you dig, darker it gets

the day

i still remember the day
you sat down
and told us
you were leaving.

the fabric beneath
my hands.
the foot tapping
on the ground.
the arm pulling
me towards
uncomfortable warmth.

the words are fuzzy.
i cannot recall which
were exchanged,
simply that they were
cruel and unfair.

one minute
you were there.
the next
you were fleeing
out the door.

girls and boys

as a child,
i was told
to smile more.
to try not to snore.
to sit upright
and not look
at the floor.

i was taught
to be quiet and polite.
to not get into fights.
to not speak out of
turn even if i was right.

the list of things
i should
or should not do
seemed to
go on forever.

never do this.
never do that.

a constant pressure
hovering over me
to ensure i was
a good little girl.

though the boys
were allowed to
make noise,
play with toys

they were sure
to destroy.

they seemed
to be given
all the power,
whilst we were left
to clean up their mess.

it's worse now
that i'm older.
everything i see
as a strength
can be turned
into a weakness
simply with a man
opening his mouth.

and although i try
to be heard,
his eyes wander south,
not hearing a word.

but that's apparently fine
because his opinion
is always right.
where mine
is always wrong.

olivia eloise sever

disappointment

every time i wake up,
i'm disappointed.
i go to bed hoping,
praying,
i will be peacefully
taken away in my sleep.

but it never happens.
cause if it did
i'd no longer feel
the pain that allows me
to write these words.

normal apologies

i'm so sorry.
i'm so sorry i'm this way.
i'm so fucking sorry.
all i do is fuck shit up
and make everything more difficult.
i'm so sorry.
i wish i was different.
i wish i wasn't me.
i wish i was good.
great.
nice.
fine.
pretty.
polite.
proper.
normal.

olivia eloise sever

freedom in death

i embed the knife
deep inside.
watch as the black
seeps out.
i've done it.
i've finally done it.
i've killed the sadness.
it's dead,
gone,
no longer.
i'm finally *free*.
i feel so light,
so nice.
cool washes over me.
my eyes fall shut.
muscles relax.
i did it,
i'm finally *free*.

fuck you

why should they dictate my life?
why should they have any say at all?
they have no part in this,
no place,
no voice.
they're not my mother.
they're not my father.
what do they think?
i'll roll over and comply?
i'll give in and listen?
i'm not some pushover
like others.
if i recover,
it will be on my own terms.
it will not be tainted
by another's selfish reasons.
yes, i suffer
and i will continue to do so.
i guarantee it.
because i will not allow myself
to get better
for anyone other than me.

creature under the bed

the monsters i thought
were under the bed,
were really
controlling my head.

once an innocent
young girl.
turned into a
creature who
darkens the world.

anxiety is a bitch

anxiety is impossible
to describe.

how do you properly
put it into words how
this uncontrollable,
unexplainable,
fear that consumes
your entire being,
could possibly control
your every move,
your every thought,
your every action.

it sounds insane
and they'll ask,
where is it?
what does it look like?
how does it feel?
and when all you
can do is stare
blankly back at them.

they'll call you
deranged,
certifiable,
mad.
and just leave you.
all alone.
with only your anxiety
as company.

olivia eloise sever

sun & rain

i hate the sun.
i believe it puts forth
an unrealistic expectation
of warmth and happiness.

it shines high in the sky,
giving false hope
that there is a light
on the other side.

i much prefer the rain.
it's sad and gloomy,
much like me.

it gives me the freedom
to take off
my mask of false smiles
and let the tears flow.
because how can it be so wrong
when the sky is doing the very same?

hurt people

hurt people, hurt people.
an explanation
more commonly used
as an excuse.

'oh they're not bad,
they're just hurt.
you must understand.'

oh, *i* understand.
i was so kindly given
a front row seat.

i took no part
in their pain,
yet i'm the one
who has paid.

but *hurt people, hurt people.*
so all's forgiven,
right?

that's just how it is, generations go by,
misery looming with every step.
passed from one person to the next.
no ending to the cycle in sight.

what am i to do,
i want no part.
i want to break the cycle.
but as they say,
hurt people, hurt people.

olivia eloise sever

ever wondered what if?

what if?
such a commonly asked question.

what if i'd been born a boy?
what if i had a pet cat?
what if i hadn't cut my hair?

what if, what if, what if…

the question runs through
my mind day and night.
keeps me up into
the early hours of the morning.

what if she'd been nicer?
what if he could understand?
what if they could accept me?

what if, what if, what if…

the longer it goes on,
the darker it gets.

what if i'm the problem?
what if i end up like her?
what if i wasn't alive?

what if, what if, what if…

romanticized depression

i knew it was getting bad again,
i could feel it in my bones.
something inside of me shifted
and i was met by a familiar unknown.

my bed was no longer
simply for sleep,
it became a pit
i continued to sink into deep.

i could only find
comfort in food,
yet the more i ate
the more my self-hatred grew.

friends i latched onto
for so long,
simply did not matter
and quickly they were gone.

i could not pull myself from my sheets
to go out anymore,
my energy disappeared
as darkness crept to my core.

smiles seemed to become
more difficult,
whereas frowns
soon became typical.

but i truly knew it
was getting bad again

olivia eloise sever

when i could no longer
produce laughter
and the silent tears
fell faster.

a reason for existing

c'est quoi mon
raison d'être?
what's my
reason for existing?

i don't think
i have one.
or at least
i don't deserve one.
or maybe it's just
i don't want one.

cause i don't
want to exist.
et tu ne peux pas
avoir un raison d'être
sans un raison.

the good kid

i was always
the good little girl.
the polite, well behaved
little kid.

the smart kid,
with perfect grades.
the quiet kid,
who always listened.
the shy kid,
who did as they were told.
i was always
the good kid.

i did what was instructed.
i took on extra responsibilities.
i didn't talk back.
i was *the good kid.*

till i wasn't.
till i had to endure
the consequences
of others' actions.
till my grades dropped
and was rarely seen in school.
till i fucked everything up.
no one to turn to.
no way to play the victim.

the ugly truth was revealed,
i was never *the good kid.*
i was *the scared kid.*

pretty and ugly

who would ever
choose me
over you?

you're so perfect,
sweet,
pretty,
slim.

how could i ever compare?

i'm so imperfect,
brash,
ugly,
overweight.

how could i ever
be a first-choice
when you exist
right next to me?

olivia eloise sever

one day

what i wouldn't give
for a day of peace.

even just one
where it doesn't feel
as though i'm crumbling
with every step i take.

one where
it doesn't feel like
my heart has been torn
from my chest,
yet someone is still
rooting around to find
more of me to take.

one single day
where my mind doesn't
lie, cheat or work against me.

just one day.
that's it.
just one.

escape within the pages

as i flip threw the pages,
words inked on the paper,
reading line after line.
i get lost in the fictional
reality before me.

of star-crossed lovers,
ending up together despite the odds.
of young girls escaping their abusers
and discovering their place in the world.
of people coming together,
finding true family within each other.

an escape is what it is.
an escape from the cruel world
i'm trapped in.

so i dive back into my books.
a seemingly never-ending supply
lining my walls,
snatching me from my life,
allowing me to live another's.

olivia eloise sever

wounds are never the same

open wounds take time
to heal, no matter the size.
once done, a mark is left.
it'll never be the same.

the deeper the wound,
the longer it takes,
the bigger the scar.
you'll never be the same.

a wound so deep
it's never been healed,
even though it's
had 17 years.
i'll never be the same.

giving into the sad

sadness has consumed me for so long
that i don't know who i am without it.
it started as a part of me
and before i knew it,
it swallowed me whole.

who am i without my
misery,
anxiety,
anger,
depression.

i've found comfort
within these feelings
for longer than i know.
and i don't believe
i can move on with my life
if it means turning my back on
what i've known for so long.

downfall of trying

i tried
and tried.

until.

i finally broke.

this is so body positive

i hate that voice
in the back of my head.
the one i can't quite reach
and has total control
over me.
the one that makes me eat
until i feel complete.
ignorant to the weight
added to my already
repulsive body.

i hate it with every
flicker of my being.
and i want to fight back
but that idea is
as useless as i am.
all it would take
is an enticing snack
and i'd give in
much to my chagrin.

the voice is in power
and it feels like
i'm a prisoner
in my own mind,
confined up in a tower.

olivia eloise sever

how do you win

how do you win
against an opponent
you don't even understand.

how do you win
against something
so monstrous
it destroys everything
in its wake.

how do you win
against a rival
who causes you
to crumble without
raising a hand.

how do you win
against an enemy
that knows every move
you're going to make.

how do you win
against yourself.

hope disappears

my chest feels hollow,
as though someone
has carved out my soul.
left to drown in
my own sorrow.
i'm losing all control,
i'm stuck feeling nothing,
yet everything.
i have lost the most
important parts of me.
they said i should feel free,
i disagree.
my body is sprawled
out on the floor.
i have no hope anymore.

butchered message

'the issue with the halloween decorations really upset olivia, she put a
lot of time, effort, creativity and money into her decorating plan.
she's feeling devastated that she isn't going to be able to see the result
of all her effort. this was the first thing i've seen her enthusiastic or
positive about in a long time. she wanted me to let you know she
really needs some space right now and not to talk about it or really
anything right now. she doesn't want to come across as rude but this
really hurt her emotional and is no were near ready to talk about it.'

dark whispers

the sun sets.
the moon rises.
night has finally come.

there are whispers
in the dark.

they're corrupting soules.
attempting to
dispose of the weak
and only leave
the strong.

the one willing
to do their bidding
without question.

sooner or later
enough nights
will have passed
and the sun
will never rise again.

in desperate need to see
the monster
haunting my dreams,
i rip off its hood.

the face staring
back at me,
i recognize it
immediately.

every feature is
identical to my own.
not a single sliver
of difference
between us.

the demon who has
stalked my every move,
haunted my every thought,
that has driven me
to the brink
of insanity,
is *me*.

rhymes for the mentally ill

my head is
filled with dark thoughts.
my eyes are
filled with tears ready to drop.
i dream of my death
each time i go to bed.
i hope i don't wake up
for whatever lies ahead.

maybe

i wanted to be you.
i no longer do.

i wished to become
exactly the same.
now i fear it more
than i can say.

i couldn't tell you
when all that changed.
when exactly you went
from hero to villain.
when our bond
became so strained
it finally broke.

maybe it was the first time
you yelled till i cried,
and didn't care
that i went to bed
with tears in my eyes.

maybe it was all the names
you called me,
that i still carry with me
to this day.

or maybe it was when
i finally stopped believing
you could be the mom
i so desperately needed.

infectious envy

i wish you never came back.
i wish you weren't here.
i know it sounds selfish
but there's so much of me
that just does not care.

cause as you stand there
in all your glory,
i'm cast off to the side,
hidden and blocked,
by your overarching shadow.

olivia eloise sever

slipping away

slowly slipping
through my fingers.
the ghost of who
i once was.

gone forever.

fault

it's always my fault,
isn't it?
there's no other
way around it.
i'm always the one
who messes up.
no matter what.

it seems like
everything i do is wrong,
or just not enough.
regardless of how long
i've been trying,
i'm not strong
enough.

i really am trying,
i swear.

but that doesn't matter,
does it?
cause this is what
i deserve.
all of this
is warranted.
cause it's always
my fault.
no matter what.

olivia eloise sever

why?

a mother is meant to
protect you from harm.
keep you safe.
love you.

yet why am i here?
sat in the corner.
tears hitting the page.
wishing i was dead.

stopped

i learnt to
muffle my cries
and fake my smiles.

i learnt to
put on a good front
and keep my mouth shut.

i learnt to
cover my scars
and keep my feelings
in a jar.

i hid from view
and didn't share my issues.
and when finally i tried
i was denied.

so i stopped.

i stopped trying.
i stopped smiling.
i stopped fighting.
i stopped living.
all in the hopes of dying.

olivia eloise sever

darkest, dark, darkness

i took it
for granted,
played with it
like a toy.
let the dark
float through my fingers
and around my head.
oblivious to the damage
it started to create.

soon the dark
encased the tips
of my fingers.
and every day the black
inconspicuously crept
further up my arm.

my once playful game
soon infected
my entire being.
no matter what i tried,
it wouldn't stop,
refused to even slow.

soon it reached
my brain,
my heart,
taking complete control.
all that was left was
darkness.

apparent affection

why is it
when boys
are mean
it's seen
as affection?

mothers tell us
they're not bullies,
they just like you.
a warped lesson
they try to ingrain
in our brains.

since when has
love meant abuse?
that showing
affection is
meant to be cruel?

why is this
a message
taught to young
girls at all?

olivia eloise sever

anger

can't you understand
that when she's mad
she loses all control.

vile words coated in hate.
hurled across the room,
with such distaste.

she doesn't mean what
she says,
regrets every phrase.
though she can't stop
when only
a monster remains.

a creature so wicked,
so monstrous,
so evil,
it can only come
from one place.

fulled by her self-hatred,
her embarrassment,
her desperation.

the vicious words spoken
conceal the unspoken.
because anger is easier to feel
and sadness is too real.

finale draft

i held on as long as i possibly could, but i've had enough.
i cannot handle anything anymore. i'm so so sorry.
i wish i could've been stronger, held on longer.
it's no one's fault but my own, please don't blame yourself.
i simply couldn't handle the pain any longer and i needed an out.
so i took one. the easy one. the cowards one.
whatever you want to call it, i've taken it because i needed to.
i didn't make this decision lightly, i didn't make it on a whim.
this was truly the only solution i found.
i wish there was a way this wouldn't cause you pain and i'm sorry
you have to deal with this.
but i had to be selfish and i pray, that one day, you can forgive me.
i truly fought as long as i could,
but i guess everyone has their breaking point.
and i reached mine.
i love you.
please remember that.
that's never changed and never will.
i love you so much and i'm so very sorry.

– a girl who lost her battle

boo feelings

i wish i had the luxury
of no longer loving you.
to be able to disregard
the feelings i hold for you.
to not be burdened by
the instinct to forgive you.

because it *hurts*.

the love i have for you
pains my very soul.

i wish i could deny that
without you i don't feel whole.
yet it seems as though
every day the ache grows.

would you even realize?

i don't think
you realize how much
i love you.

how if it
wasn't for you,
i would've been gone
a long time ago.

i don't think
you realize
the impact
you have on me.

how i could simply
look at you
and i'd smile.

i don't think
you realize how much
i cherish our time together.

how i could easily sit
and listen to you
for hours
and never grow bored.

but that's the problem.
you don't realize.
you don't realize
how much you mean to me
and it causes me to question

olivia eloise sever

if i even mean anything
to you at all.

if things were different
we wouldn't even
know each other.

i know i would feel the absence,
but would *you*?
would you even notice?
would you even realize?

get out.

depression is like an old friend,
who you let crash on your couch.
yet they overstay their welcome
and won't clear out.

the easter bunny

my earliest memory
was watching my parents
argue over an easter basket
through the sliver under
my door.

i think about that a lot.
how common it was
for me to be lulled asleep
by the sounds of yelling.

but that's not what
stuck out with
this memory.

i was only 4 years old
and cause my parents
couldn't simply get along
for a least one night,
i found out the truth.

the easter bunny isn't real.

everything right

i did everything right.
i did what i was told.
i played the part
you put before me
perfectly.

i did everything right.
i didn't defy you.
i listened and obeyed
like a puppet hung
on a chain.
ready for a show.

i did everything right.
i was the perfect little girl.
i stayed polite and quiet
as though i were a doll
displayed on
the highest shelf.

used as a pawn
in your bitter wars.

constantly redrawn
to fit the monster you need.

no regard for what
i've undergone.

i did everything right.
yet i'm somehow in the wrong.

life, death, living, suicide

life.
my life.
refusing my death.
purely existing.
it has no purpose
if you simply sit still,
stay in one place,
stagnant in time.

death.
my death.
taking my life.
it's all i have left.
the only thing i want.
i don't want to be alive,
i want to be dead,
lifeless, unmoving.

living.
i'm terrified of it,
i'm not kidding.
get up,
live,
sleep.
an ever-tiring repetition
i want no part of.

suicide.
i'm terrified of it,
i'm not joking.
it scares me so deep,
i can feel it inside.

yet the want is still there.
everlasting,
all-consuming,
never-ending.

when rage spills

'how are you?'

'i'm fine.'

i'm not fine,
not even close.
i want to rip
my skin off.
cut until i hit bone.
see the blood
pour out.
watch the sheets
stain beneath me.
as if it'll alleviate
the pain in my head,
even a little bit,
even the tiniest amount.

but i don't say that
or else i'll be met
by horrified faces
and disgusted expressions.
so instead i plaster on
the largest smile
i can muster and say,

'i'm fine.'

closed off

you call me closed off.
yet every time i let
someone in,
i lose another
part of me.
and eventually
i will have no more to give
and everything will be gone.

black, blue and broken

my soul
hurts.

it's bruised
and broken.

beyond repair.

i want my mom

i want my mom.
a sentence i say
to myself every day.

crying.
i want my mom.

lonely.
i want my mom.

angry.
i want my mom.

but really
i don't want *my* mom,
i want *a* mom.

someone who would
love and care for me,
not just a roommate
you see occasionally.

someone who would
treat me as her daughter,
not just an extension
of herself.

so maybe i should
change the phrase,
i don't want *my* mom.
i just want *a* mom.

love of pain

i like hurting myself.
i like cutting.
i don't know why,
i haven't a clue.
but i also hate it.
i don't like pain,
i have a very low tolerance.
yet here i am adding to the lines,
blood running down my arm.
i couldn't tell you why,
i haven't a clue.
i simply like it.
the feeling,
the clarity,
the numbness,
the silence.
there's more to it than just pain.
there's comfort,
peace,
tranquillity,
euphoria.
so yes,
i hate it,
yet i love it at the same time.

unworthy

i wish you never had me,
for both my sake
and your own.

you should've never
been a *mother*.
you were never worthy
of that title.

your martyr act
grew old fast.
yet the world continued
to buy into it.

you took away
my privacy,
my control.
blamed me for
your own faults
and wrongdoings.

i never got the apology
i deserve,
didn't even get a chance
to fight back.

i was just a child
who deserved a mother.
you were just a mother
who never deserved a child.

olivia eloise sever

pointless.

i think life is pointless
and cruel.
we are put on this earth
with the promise
of love and happiness.

yet that is a lie.

all this world has done
is bring me pain and misery.

why should i continue to live
when the only thing
that is guaranteed
is the preservation
of my sadness?

those few fleeting moments
of delight
are not worth
the continuance of my suffering.

the kindred spirits of a girl and her doll

ivory skin cracking
under the pressure.
much like the porcelain doll
on my shelf.
and i ask myself,
how much longer
till i'm missing pieces
that can never be replaced,
much like she is.

from a young girl to the first man she ever loved

where are you?
where have you gone?
where is the man who
played princesses with me?
where is the man who
held me when i cried?
where is the man who
gave me hope when i was
hidden away, trapped?

you were my hero,
now i can't even look at you.
i know it's not fair.
i know it's not right.
yet you are unaware
of the resentment
i hold towards you.
of the anger brewing
beneath my skin.
burning that only goes away
when the tears start to fall.

you are no longer
who i remember.
maybe it's my fault
that i saw you in such
a positive light.
that i latched onto you
with such might.
too blinded from
protecting myself against
the trauma caused

by another,
to see you were hurting me too,
just in a different way.

or maybe you are that great.
maybe i'm the one in the wrong.
that i've messed up
for so long,
i am in dire need
to blame another
for my own faults.

or maybe it's simply
that i've grown up
and i'm caught in a slump.
but i'll never stop wondering,
where are you?
where have you gone?

olivia eloise sever

duology of mine

'i'm doing great'
 i'm not doing great

'everything is fine'
 nothing is fine

'i'm living life to the fullest'
 i wish i were dead

rhyming questions

if you saw me
as i see myself,
would you understand?
or would you run
the first chance you had.

if you could
see inside my head,
would you accept all the bad?
or would you call me crazy?
my feelings be damned.

haunting regret

i am continuously haunted
by memories of my dead mother,
of horrible fights with my father,
of scars that cover my body
and the blood that once poured from them.
of plans, i wish i had gone through with
that could've stopped my beating heart.
day and night
my mind is tormented,
never to be stopped.
no matter how much i've pleaded.

comforting rain

i stared at your grave
for a long while,
with tears streaming
down my face.

as if the world
could feel my pain,
the clouds darkened
and it started to rain.

and for a moment
it made me feel
less alone.

olivia eloise sever

deeper you dig, darker it gets

olivia eloise sever

to the reader,

this is my soul on paper, a comfort during my worst times.
crack open my heart, let it bleed out and this is what would be left.
thoughts i never considered i'd outlive, put into words.

i still struggle. i still get stuck in the dark.
there are days that are good. there are days that are bad.
it's not linear. there are downs. but also ups.
i fight every day to find the light.
but i am glad i am here for that fight.
i am glad i did not take my life.
i am glad i am alive.

if you found your thoughts looking back at you within these pages.
you are not alone. you are valid.
i am glad you are here to read these words.
and i hope you stick around.

                                            -thank you

deeper you dig, darker it gets

Printed in Great Britain
by Amazon

36068834R00066